Celebrating your year

1970

a very special year for

_____

_____

_____

_____

_____

A message from the author:

Welcome to the year 1970.

I trust you will enjoy this fascinating romp down memory lane.

And when you have reached the end of the book, please join me in the battle against AI generated copy-cat books and fake reviews.

Details are near the back of the book.

Best regards,
Bernard Bradforsand-Tyler.

Contents

1970 Family Life in the USA 8
Life in the United Kingdom 12
Hippies and the Rise of the Communes 16
Anti-Vietnam War Sentiment 19
Kent State University Shootings 21
Apollo 13 Failed Moon Mission 22
Inaugural Jumbo Jet Flight 25
Our Love Affair with Automobiles 28
Clean Air for All 32
Introducing Earth Day 34
The First Pride Parades 37
    Tuning in to Television 39
    Sesame Street Hits Our Screens 44
    1970 in Cinema and Film 46
    Top Grossing Films of the Year 47
A Decade of Disasters 48
Musical Memories 50
1970 Billboard Top 30 Songs 52
    Fashion Trends of the 1970s 56
    Schwarzenegger Wins Mr. Olympia 64
    British Commonwealth Games 65
    Also in Sports 66
Other News from 1970 70
Famous People Born in 1970 72
1970 in Numbers 76
Image Attributions 84

Advertisement

Simplicity says it's shocking!

Shocking jolts of Rit color really turn satin on. You tie, dip and dye it to create your own unique print. Sew on electrifying Simplicity Pattern! Rit color makes it fun–Simplicity Patterns make it easy–you make it different from anyone else!

Crumple an area of fabric together. Tuck knot center inside. Secure with rubber bands.

Plot the "knots" over the fabric.

Dip whole fabric of just knots in simmering diluted Rit for 15 mins. ¼ cup of liquid Rit or ½ pkg regular Powder Rit to each qt water.

Rinse in running water. Untie knots. Re-rinse till water runs clear. Iron damp.

Make your Simplicity fashion. This is the basic tie-dye method. To achieve different effects write to Rit Tie-Dye. PO Box 307. Coventry, Conn. 06238.

Let's flashback to 1970, a very special year.

Was this the year you were born?

Was this the year you were married?

Whatever the reason, this book is a celebration of your year,

THE YEAR 1970.

Turn the pages to discover a book packed with fun-filled fabulous facts. We look at the people, the places, the politics and the pleasures that made 1970 unique and helped shape the world we know today.

So get your time-travel suit on, and enjoy this trip down memory lane, to rediscover what life was like, back in the year 1970.

1970 Family Life in the USA

Imagine if time-travel was a reality, and one fine morning you wake up to find yourself flashed back in time, back to the year 1970.

What would life be like for a typical family, in a typical town, somewhere in America?

Young couple at May Day rally, 1st May 1970, Yale, USA.

By the start of the '70s our cultural gaze had shifted away from London's Swinging Sixties, back to the USA. The hippie view of the world, with its emphasis on peace, love and nature, focused our collective attention on the anti-war and anti-pollution movements.

We were fed-up with the ongoing Cold War and the draining war in Vietnam. We were ready for a new focus and a new vision. The counterculture movements of the late '60s continued well into the 1970s, as we rejected the old traditions and conservative values of our parents. Women, African Americans, LGBT communities and environmentalists would ramp up the fight for recognition and equality.

In the ten years to 1970, the US population had increased by 12% to 209.5 million.[1] The first of the Baby Boomers were now a vocal population of young adults. Birth rates and family sizes were falling, thanks to changing family values and readily available contraceptives.

Women's Strike for Equality march, 26th Aug 1970, New York, USA.

At the same time divorce rates were rising. The feminist movement had left women more educated and confident. As no-fault divorce laws came into effect, couples could legally divorce for any or no reason at all. An estimated 50% of couples who married in 1970 would end up divorced in future years.[2]

Levels of education had also increased–76.9% of 17-year-olds graduated high school in 1970 (up from 69.5% ten years earlier).[3] A further 37.3% of 18 to 19-year-olds continued to a higher education institution (up from 23.6%).[4]

[1] worldometers.info/world-population.
[2] nationalaffairs.com/publications/detail/the-evolution-of-divorce.
[3] usafacts.org/data/topics/people-society/education.
[4] statista.com/statistics/236093/higher-education-enrollment-rates-by-age-group-us.

Advertisement

Natural Menthol Blend
(means naturally fresh taste)
Salem's unique blend features natural menthol, not the kind made in laboratories. Like our superb tobaccos, our menthol is naturally grown. You'll get a taste that's not harsh or hot... a taste as naturally cool and fresh as Springtime.

Did you know that the term "generation gap" was coined by the Baby Boomers to describe the differences between their attitudes and values, and those of their old-world parents? This new generation questioned everything about "the American Dream", expressing their social and political views through their fashion, literature, music and art.

A family portrait, 1970.

Universities and colleges became breeding grounds for free-thinking, liberal theories. Students often shared accommodation, partly for convenience and cost savings, but also as an expression of a new way of living, cohabiting, exploring sexual freedoms and spiritual fulfillment.

College students on campus, 1970.

In 1970 the median family income was $9,870 a year.[1] Unemployment stood at 6.1%, with GDP growth at 0.2%.[2]

Average costs in 1970 [3]	
New house	$24,844
New car	$3,430
Television	$740
A gallon of gasoline	$0.35

[1] census.gov/library/publications/1971/demo/p60-80.html.
[2] thebalance.com/unemployment-rate-by-year-3305506.
[3] thepeoplehistory.com.

Life in the United Kingdom

Now just imagine you flashed back to a town in 1970 England. Although not all doom and gloom, the United Kingdom had found itself slipping on the world stage as America and the USSR battled for domination.

London had reigned as the center of global culture during the decade of the '60s, but by 1970 the shine had mostly faded. The joyful, carefree optimism of England's Swinging Sixties could not last forever.

Above and below: London street scenes in 1970.

The sentiment on the streets had shifted from frivolity to revolution. This mood was echoed in the fashion, art and culture of the time. In music especially, popular American musicians were penning lyrics encouraging people worldwide to challenge authority, to stand up for their rights and demand change.

The feminist movement had a long-established history in Britain, and it continued to gain in force. 1970 saw the First National Women's Liberation Conference being held in Oxford, and the passing of the Equal Pay Act.

However women were still expected to be the main caregiver at home, despite many having full time jobs.

Protestors at the first Women's Liberation Movement march, 8th March 1971.

The average age of marriage for women was 24.7, with 50% of married women having their first child before turning 25.[1]

The average fertility rate was 2.4 (births per woman), down from a peak of 2.9 in 1964.[1] The contraceptive pill (available since 1961) and the legalisation of abortion (1967) aided in this decline.

Family on a Chelsea street, Nov 1970.

By 1970, less than 50% of families owned a car.[2] Within the larger cities, most people commuted by public transport.

10% of homes did not have internal toilets, while 9% were still without baths. 58% lacked telephones and 66% lacked central heating.[3]

Only 33% of 18-year-olds finished high school, a figure far lower than most other industrialized nations.

[1] ons.gov.uk/peoplepopulationandcommunity.
[2&3] ons.gov.uk/ons/rel/ghs/general-lifestyle- survey/2011/rpt-40-years.html

Advertisement

It's cold.
It's inhuman.
But it gives you £10.

The National Westminster at 46 Regent Street, Swindon, now has a Cash Dispenser. It delivers £10, day or night, to any National Westminster customer with a cashcard.

National Westminster's new Cash Dispensers have become so popular that we're now putting them in as fast as we can.

It's certainly nice to know there's always £10 waiting for you whenever you need it—day or night, seven days a week.

You simply feed in your cashcard, tap out your number, and it hands out the money without a murmur.

By the end of last year there were more than 200 machines around the country. This year we are putting in a lot more.

We're doing all we can to make our service as friendly and personal as we can. But this is one case where we don't think you'll mind a machine taking over.

After all—who cares how impersonal it is, as long as it comes across with the money?

National Westminster Bank
Our roots are our branches

It's cold. it's inhuman. But it gives you £10

The National Westminster at 46 Regent Street, Swindon, now has a Cash Dispenser. It delivers £10, day or night, to any National Westminster customer with a cashcard.

National Westminster's new Cash Dispensers have become so popular that we're now putting them in as fast as we can.

It's certainly nice to know there's always £10 waiting for you whenever you need it–day or night, seven days a week.

You simply feed in your cashcard, tap out your number, and it hands out the money without a murmur.

By the end of last year there were more than 200 machines around the country. This year we are putting in a lot more.

We're doing all we can to make our service as friendly and personal as we can. But this is one case where we don't think you'll mind a machine taking over.

After all–who cares how impersonal it is, as long as it comes across with money?

National Westminster Bank   Our roots are our branches

By 1970, the UK was nearly half-way through repaying its post-war loans from America and Canada. The 20-year post-war building boom, which had kept cash flowing and unemployment low, was over.

Economic growth in the UK was only half that of France and Germany, with annual GDP having slipped from 2nd place in 1960 (behind only USA), to 5th place in 1970. Moreover, UK GDP per capita had slipped to 23rd place in world rankings.[1]

The UK Postal Workers strike.

By 1970, most of the former colonies of the United Kingdom had been granted their independence. The cost to keep and defend them had proven too high a burden to carry.

Industrial strife was high, inflation was on the rise, political violence in Northern Ireland was escalating. England in 1970 was a country in decline. And the worse was yet to come.

The decade ahead would bring a mounting series of economic crises, industrial actions and major political battles.

Women's Liberation Movement protest, 1970.

British soldiers hold back Northern Ireland protestors, 1970.

[1] nationmaster.com/country-info/stats/Economy/GDP.

Hippies and the Rise of the Communes   1960s–1970s

By the early '70s, the Baby Boomers were young adults. Everything about them was a break-away from their parents: their music, their fashion, their values, their personal and sexual freedoms. They were non-traditional, non-conformists, anti-authority, anti-consumerist, anti-war, politically active, experimental drug users, hippies, believers and disbelievers. Anything was possible. Everything was acceptable.

The "Back to the Land" movement and the rise of communal living in the late '60s and early '70s were lifestyle expressions of freedom of choice. Communes were anti-establishment and experimental, communes were whatever the inhabitants chose them to be. Up to 3000 communes existed in the USA during this period.[1]

In the state of Vermont, a haven for hippies, an estimated one third of young adults (below age 34) were living communally.[2]

[1&2] forbes.com/sites/russellflannery/2021/04/11/what-happened-to-americas-communes/?sh=7454bc05c577

Most communes encouraged co-ownership of possessions, collective chores and shared child-raising. For many, clothes, monogamy and drug usage were optional. By rejecting the 40-hour work week, many communards relied on food stamps, or temporary odd jobs to keep themselves nourished.

In rural areas communards practiced living off the land, setting up farms, building their own houses and selling handicrafts.

Myrtle Hill Farm, Vermont.

A geodesic dome house built at Myrtle Hill Farm, Vermont. Recalls one communard, "In 1971 a young man named Bernie Sanders visited Myrtle Hill Farm... Sanders' tendency to just sit around talking politics and avoid actual physical labor got him the boot."[1]

Communards at Hog Farm, California.

The rise of communal living in the late '60s and early '70s was worldwide. Although the vast majority only survived a few years, some communes continue to exist today.

[1] From *We Are As Gods: Back to the Land in the 1970s on the Quest for a New America* by Brian Doherty.

Advertisement

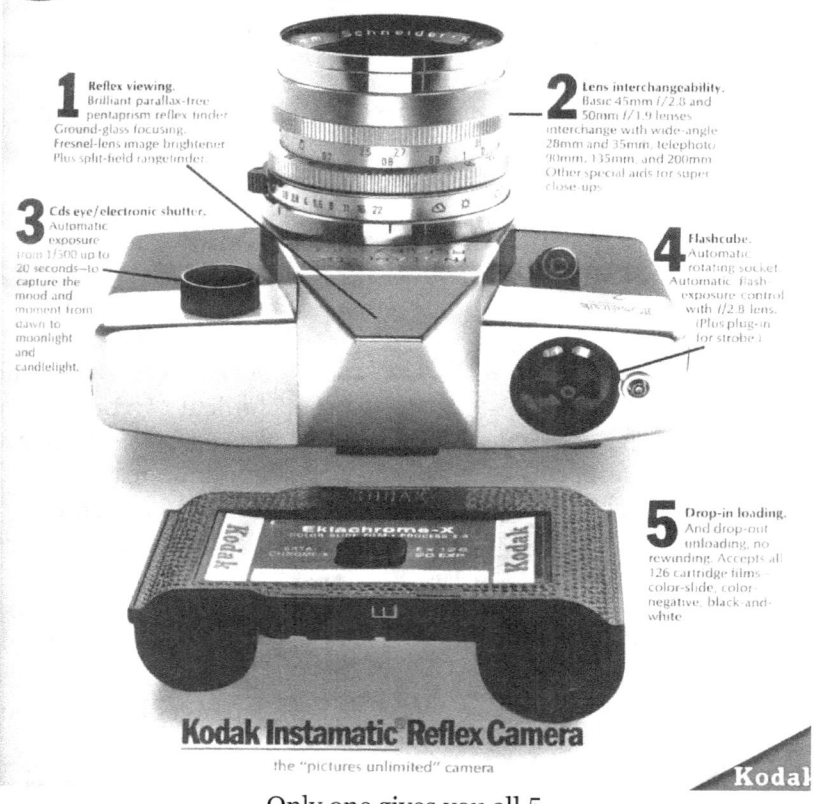

Only one gives you all 5

1 Reflex viewing. Brilliant parallax-free pentaprism reflex finder. Ground-glass focusing. Fresnel-lens image brightener. Plus split-field rangefinder.

2 Lens interchangeability. Basic 45mm $f/2.8$ and 50mm $f/1.9$ lenses interchange with wide-angle 28mm and 35mm, telephoto 90mm, 135mm and 200mm. Other special aids for super close-ups.

3 Cds eye/electronic shutter. Automatic exposure from 1/500 up to 20 seconds–to capture the mood and moment from dawn to moonlight and candlelight.

4 Flashcube. Automatic rotating socket. Automatic flash-exposure control with $f/2.8$ lens. (Plus plug-in for strobe.)

5 Drop-in loading. And drop-out unloading, no rewinding. Accepts all 126 cartridge films– color-slide, color-negative, black-and-white.

Kodak Instamatic Reflex Camera   the "picture unlimited" camera

Anti-Vietnam War Sentiment 1955-1975

We had long ago grown tired and fed-up with the ongoing Vietnam War (known in Vietnam as the American War). By 1970, the US still had 334,600 troops stationed in Vietnam (38% less than two years earlier), with an additional 67,000 allied troops from South Korea, Thailand, Australia and New Zealand.[1]

Anti-war sentiment had been escalating during the previous few years, as more and more protestors took to the streets to demonstrate against what they believed to be an immoral war.

Anti-Vietnam War protestors, circa 1970-'71.

In 1970, actress Jane Fonda began speaking out against American involvement in the Vietnam War. She would become the war's most high-profile critic, earning her the nickname "Hanoi Jane".

Forced to fight a war they didn't believe in, morale among the draftees was low. Drug usage became rampant. It is estimated up to 50% of US soldiers experimented with marijuana, opium and heroin, cheaply available on the streets of Saigon. US military hospitals would later report drug abuse victims far outnumbered actual war casualties.

[1] americanwarlibrary.com/vietnam/vwatl.htm

Clairol frees the 'fro

A Kindness Instant Hairsetter styles it high, wide and easy to comb, in just 15 minutes. Without hot combs or harsh chemicals.

This side was shaped with a comb.

This side was set with the Kindness Spray-and-Roll System.

Kent State University Shootings

4th May 1970

On 4th May 1970, Ohio National Guardsmen opened fire on protesters, killing four students and wounding nine others at Kent State University, Ohio. The students had been demonstrating against US bombing incursions into Cambodia, as an extension of America's involvement in the Vietnam War.

The general public and members of congress argued that President Nixon had expanded the war illegally. The students were unarmed.

Ohio National Guardsmen open fire on unarmed students, Kent State University, 4th May 1970.

The ensuing outrage sparked student strikes across the country. More than 400 colleges and universities joined in, many shutting down completely during the strikes. Four million students took part, consolidating further the public's opinion against US continued involvement in the Vietnam War.

Apollo 13 Failed Moon Mission   11th April 1970

Launch of Apollo 13 and The Apollo 13 crew prior to boarding.

Apollo 13 was to be the third manned mission to the moon, following the successful 1969 moon landings of Apollo 11 and Apollo 12. It launched on 11th April from the Kennedy Space Center, Florida. Onboard were commander James A. Lovell, Jr., and pilots John L. Swigert, Jr. and Fred W. Haise, Jr.

56 hours after take-off, the astronauts heard a "pretty loud bang" during routine stirring of the cryogenic tanks. Communication to Earth was momentarily cut, automatically reconnecting to transmit the legendary words from Swigert, then Lovell, "Houston, we've had a problem..."

Evening news headlines, 12th April 1970.

In the minutes after the explosion the crew noticed oxygen tanks 1 and 2 emptying, and from the window they could see gas a leaking out. The pressure caused by the releasing oxygen resulted in a series of technical failures occurring in quick succession, including separation of an outer panel and damage to the antenna.

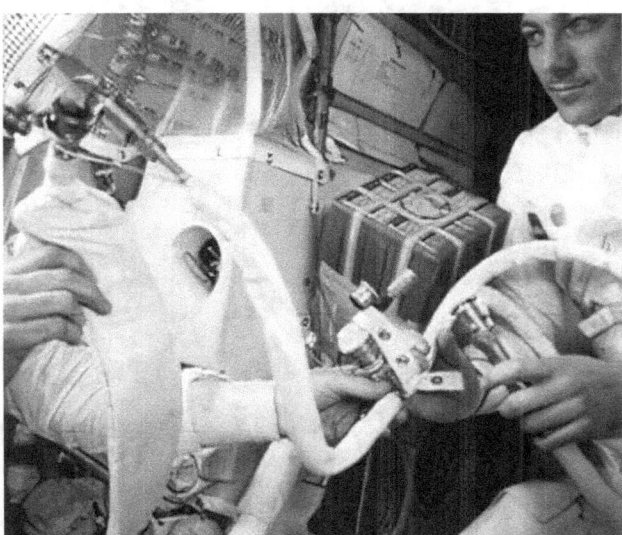

Limited oxygen meant limited ability to generate electricity and produce water. The crew worked with mission control to preserve what little oxygen they had, to extract carbon dioxide, and to ensure sufficient electricity for the re-entry.

Apollo astronauts with their "mail box", a make-shift CO_2 filter created with materials on-hand, for purging carbon dioxide from the Lunar Module.

Orbiting around the moon without landing, the crippled Apollo 13 returned to Earth six days after take-off.

40 million Americans and millions more worldwide watched Apollo 13's splashdown in the South Pacific.

Astronauts Haise, Lovell and Swigert (left to right) aboard carrier Iwo Jima after their rescue, 17th April 1970.

Advertisement

747 INTRODUCES NEW LOOK IN COMFORT AND SERVICE

When Pan Am places the first 362-passenger 747 in commercial service, air travel will enter a new phase in terms of service and speed, comfort and convenience. The 747 will be the largest, fastest and most luxurious airliner in the history of aviation. The interior of the 747 creates the atmosphere of a living room in the sky with roomy seats, extra-wide aisles, thick carpeting, high ceiling, six galleys, 12 rest rooms, six separate movie screens and an upper deck lounge.

Dome-shaped lounge on upper deck of 747 features swivel seats and banquettes.

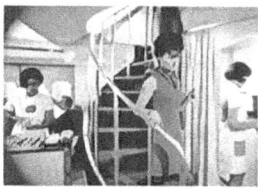
Circular stairway leads from First Class section to lounge on upper deck

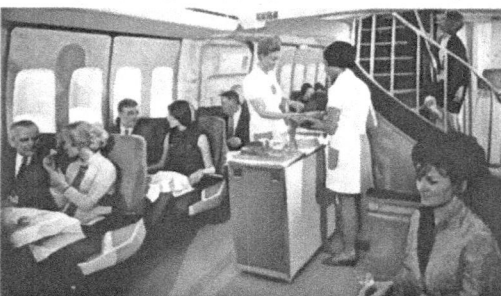
First Class in 747 resembles salon with service bar and roomy two-seat units

Two 20-inch wide aisles run full length of Economy section

Pan Am's 747 Theater-in-the-Air has advanced large-screen color system

The 747 will provide economy passengers with greater comfort than ever before possible. Economy seats in 747 are 10 per cent wider than in 707

747 introduces the new look in comfort and service

When Pan Am places the first 362-passenger 747 in commercial service, air travel will enter a new phase in terms of service and speed, comfort and convenience. The 747 will be the largest, fastest and most luxurious airliner in the history of aviation. The interior of the 747 creates the atmosphere of a living room in the sky with roomy seats, extra-wide aisles, thick carpeting, high ceiling, six galleys, 12 rest rooms, six separate movie screens and an upper deck lounge.

Dome-shaped lounge on upper deck of 747 features swivel seats and banquettes.

Circular stairway leads from First Class section to lounge on upper deck.

First Class in 747 resembles salon with service bar and roomy two-seat units.

Two 20-inch wide aisles run full length of Economy section.

Pan Am's 747 Theater-in-the-Air has advanced large-screen color system.

The 747 will provide economy passengers with greater comfort than ever before possible. Economy seats in 747 are 10 percent wider than in 707.

Inaugural Jumbo Jet Flight

22nd January 1970

On 22nd January 1970, the first Jumbo Jet commercial flight took place, carrying 352 passengers and 20 crew members from New York to London. Originally scheduled for take off on the evening before, a malfunction in one of the engines caused the historic Boeing 747 flight for Pan Am to be delayed by six hours. Passengers had to disembark and wait for a replacement jet.

The Boeing 747, first public preview.

Constructed in just 16 months, the wide-body dual-aisle aircraft required a team of 50,000 mechanics, engineers, construction workers and staff to create the worlds "largest civilian airplane", a title it held till the creation of the A380 in 2007.

Boeing has sold over 1,500 passenger and cargo 747s, with about 500 still in service today.

The 747 has "starred" in numerous Hollywood films including *Airport 1975*, *Airport '77*, and *Air Force One*.

Deregulation of the airline industry has shifted focus to efficiency over service, favoring smaller twin-engine aircraft and reducing demand for the jumbo giants. In 2017 Boeing stopped making 747s for passenger use. They are however, still in demand as long-haul freight carriers.

Advertisement

When they're looking up to you, are they really looking down at you?

When they're looking up to you, are they really looking down at you?

The station wagon on the left is known in some circles as a status symbol.

The station wagon on the right is known in the same circles as a mistake.

Now the status symbol is long and low and really quite beautiful. Whereas the Volkswagen is short and high and really quite ugly.

The status symbol features a powerful engine. A Volkswagen engine is not as powerful, but it'll go farther on a gallon of gas.

The status symbol boasts roughly 88 cubic feet of carrying space. The Volkswagen has twice that amount. 176 cubic feet.

Conclusion: If you're looking for something to show how big you are, then we suggest you get yourself a status symbol. But if you're looking for something that's just plain big, then maybe it wasn't us who made the mistake after all.

Advertisement

Dodge Challenger...The sports car that knows how to treat a lady.

If you didn't know better, you'd almost think Challenger had been designed by a woman. Who else would have made it low and sporty-looking, but still big enough so you don't get that squashed feeling when you're inside? Aren't things like the sports-type steering wheel and color-coordinated carpeting women's touches? Who but a member of the female sex would be smart enough to combine looks with practicality? Take those flush door handles. They aren't just for looks, you know. They're safer, too. And those thrifty standard six- and eight-cylinder engines. Both use regular gas. Speaking of thrift, Challenger's price is pretty nice, too. If Challenger was designed by a man, I bet he talked to his wife first.

If you think all this was worth waiting for...you could be Dodge material.

Our Love Affair with Automobiles

Our love affair with automobiles began back in the early '50s, and by 1970 we were irreversibly addicted to our vehicles. Americans owned an average of 1.5 cars per family. Automobile numbers had risen 45% during the preceding 10 years. Although car costs had risen markedly, so too had real wages. The cost of a standard family car was equivalent to one-third the average family income (dropping from half the average family income in 1960).

Six car-producing countries dominated the industry in 1970: Japan, Germany, England, France and Italy, with America in the top spot.

Japan's recent rise into this elite group had been particularly aggressive, and their compact cars stood poised to dominate the world markets.

Live below your means.

Volkswagen's Beetle remained popular, as it had been throughout the 1960s.

Italian style, French soul, International muscle.

The New Peugeot 504

Imports of foreign cars now made up 14% of American new car sales. Foreign cars were generally more compact and fuel efficient than the American muscle cars.

Detroit was America's car manufacturing powerhouse, where "the Big Three" (Ford, General Motors and Chrysler) produced the bulk of cars sold. Although still renowned for their gas-guzzling muscle cars, pressure from imports and domestic demand for more compact, fuel-efficient cars, led to a general downsizing. Compact and sub-compact cars sales grew, increasing markedly after the Arab embargo oil crisis of 1973.

Advertisement

If you can afford a car you can afford two Gremlins.

Credit:
HEIMANN, Jim
70's All-American Ads
Taschen
via Barraclou.com

American Motors

If you can afford a car you can afford two Gremlins.

Until April 1, 1970, only an imported economy car could make that statement.

Then American Motors introduced the Gremlin. And America had a car priced to compete with the imports. The two-passenger Gremlin lists for $1,879, the four-passenger for $1,959.

The Gremlin gets the best mileage of any car made in America. It goes about 500 miles on a tank of gas. It normally goes 6,000 miles between oil changes, 24,000 between lube jobs.

From bumper to bumper, it's just $2^1/_2$ inches longer than a Volkswagen. Yet its turning circle is 3 feet less than VW's. Which makes the Gremlin about the easiest car in the world to park and handle.

For a car this size, the Gremlin does surprisingly well on expressways. It is 10 inches wider, 7 inches lower and 765 pounds heavier than a VW, which means a smoother more stable ride. And its 128 hp engine goes from 0 to 60 in 15.3 seconds.

Aside from all these practical advantages, the Gremlin gives you something no imported economy car could ever offer.

The fun of driving the new American car.

Advertisement

455 cubic inches powerful. Isn't that the way you want luxury to be?
Make this simple test before you answer.
   Open the hood of a 1970 Bonneville. Now, if you can't resist a low whistle or gasp—merely at the sight of the resident 360-hp V-8—your answer is "Yes". Or...
   Take the wheel. (Getting in you just might have noticed the richly patterned fabrics and appointments our competitors are so concerned about. But we digress.) OK. Turn the key and test drive. "Responsive" may be your word for Bonneville. And that's good enough for us.
   No question, it's the most powerful—and luxurious—Bonneville we've ever built. It's at your Pontiac dealer's. Where the way it's going to be is now.

Pontiac's new Bonneville

Clean Air for All

Driver wearing a smog mask in the early '70s, Los Angeles, USA.

Our love affair with gas-guzzling, pollutant-emitting cars caused our air quality to deteriorate to severely unhealthy levels throughout the '50s and '60s. By the early '70s, pollutants from exhaust and industries left major cities regularly blanketed in a hazardous thick brown haze.

By 1972, the Clean Air Act (passed 31st December 1970) had become a serious concern for car manufacturers. The Act required leaded petrol engines to be phased out, and new vehicles to be engineered for cleaner emissions and fuel efficiency.

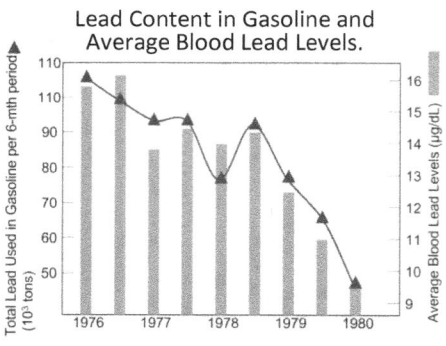

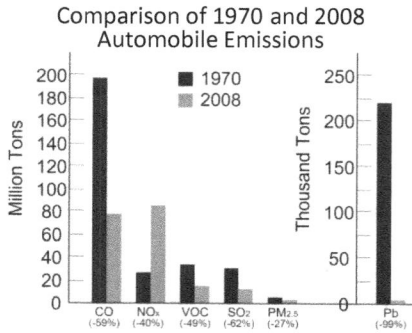

The Act required a 90% reduction of emissions from new automobiles within five years, targeting six major public health pollutants, including lead and carbon monoxide.

The US Environmental Protection Agency gave the states a short five years to meet these clean air quality goals, forcing the states to put pressure on industry and vehicle manufacturers.

The UK implemented their first Clean Air Act in 1956. Their revised Act of 1970 specifically targeted carbon monoxide and hydrocarbons from automobile engines.

In Canada, Australia, and across Europe, similar legislations were developed throughout the '70s to tackle the undeniable problem of automobile-created photochemical smog which affected all major cities.

Different countries set their own standards, some more stringent than others. They also created their own methods for emissions testing of vehicles prior to sale, and of air quality testing for cities.

New York aerial view in 1973 and now.

L.A. Grand Avenue in 1967 and now.

London's Great Fog of 1952 resulted in the deaths of 12,000 Londoners.

Introducing Earth Day

22nd April 1970

Throngs jamming Fifth Avenue yesterday in response to a call for the regeneration of a polluted environment. View is north from 43d Street, with Central Park in background.

When the concept for Earth Day was first proposed, we were ready for positive change. Senator Gaylord Nelson envisioned it as a national day of education about environmental concerns. He invited people from all states to get involved, and the response was overwhelming. An army of volunteers helped organize the event, working with universities, colleges and local communities. 20 million nationwide took part.

Nelson was to remark, "Earth Day worked because of the spontaneous response at the grassroots level... That was the remarkable thing about Earth Day. It organized itself."[1]

Public opinion polls the following year showed that Earth Day had succeeded in raising awareness about environmental issues.

[1] nelsonearthday.net.

In December 1970, the US Environmental Protection Agency was created. With rising awareness of environmental issues, the decade of the '70s saw many important legislative acts passed into law concerning air quality, water quality, toxic substances, mining and land reclamation, and protection of endangered species.

Environmental awareness projects at school.   Official Earth Day 2020 poster.

Earth Day has since grown into an annual global event. Nearly 200 countries take part incorporating thousands of environmental groups and more than one billion people. Celebrated for more than 50 years, Earth Day continues to focus on environmental education and advocacy, science and cleaning up the planet.

Community volunteers picking up trash.   Volunteers planting trees.

Advertisement

GETTING AWAY FROM BUSINESS IS GOOD FOR BUSINESS!

Winter is a great time for you to get away from business and relax in sunny Las Vegas. After a few days in the Nevada desert you will return to the office tan and relaxed, feeling like a leader and looking like the boss. When the secretaries stop chasing you around the desk you can tell your business associates all about your Las Vegas trip: clear desert air and moonlit nights, lavish entertainment, gourmet dining, and luxurious accommodations. You will have to stretch the truth about the cost though.....Las Vegas rates are so low you won't look like a high roller if you tell it like it is. Only your travel agent will know.

Getting away from business is good for business!

Winter is a great time for you to get away from business and relax in sunny Las Vegas. After a few days in the Nevada desert you will return to the office tan and relaxed, feeling like a leader and looking like the boss. When the secretaries stop chasing you around the desk you can tell your business associates all about your Las Vegas trip: clear desert air and moonlit nights, lavish entertainment, gourmet dining, and luxurious accommodations. You will have to stretch the truth about the cost though...Las Vegas rates are so low you won't look like a high roller if you tell it like it is. Only your travel agent will know.

Visit Las Vegas

The First Pride Parades

28th June 1970

On Saturday 27th June 1969, police stormed the Stonewall Inn, a popular gay bar, in Greenwich Village, New York. The demonstrations and riots that ensued gave rise to the formation of activist groups determined to fight for the rights of the LGBT community.

One year later, the first Pride Parades were held in New York and Los Angeles, with smaller marches across other US cities. Originally known as the Gay Liberation Marches or Gay Freedom Marches, their focus was on raising awareness for political activism and encouraging a more open and integrated LGBT community.

New York Gay Liberation march, 28th June 1970.

Five decades later, Pride Parades take place in countless cities world wide. The focus is now more celebratory and festive, incorporating floats, costumes, music and dancing.

Celebrating 50 years of Pride Parades in Norway, 2019.

Advertisement

Now the biggest breakthrough in Color TV comes in small, medium, and large

Zenith Chromacolor

Now the biggest breakthrough in Color TV comes in small, medium, and large

Last year, Zenith introduced Chromacolor, the most revolutionary color television system ever invented, featuring Zenith's famous Handcrafted chassis and patented Chromacolor picture tube. Result: a color picture that outbrightened and outdetailed every giant-screen color TV before Chromacolor!

Now Zenith announces the Chromacolor family... a complete range of Chromacolor cabinet styles and screen sizes designed to fit right into your life. All the brilliance and realism of the Chromacolor TV picture in consoles, table models and new compact fit-any-where cabinets. With a choice of 19", 23" and new giant 25" (diag.) screen sizes.

Remember: only your Zenith dealer has Chromacolor.

Tuning in to Television

The television was our must-have appliance of the '50s and '60s, taking pride of place in our family or living rooms. By 1970, 95% of US households owned a television,[1] of which more than 40% were color sets.

Around 700 TV stations and networks generated $3.6 billion in advertising revenue,[2] (equivalent to $60 billion today).

Elsewhere in the world, rates of television ownership lagged behind the USA. In many countries, television networks were government owned or subsidized, allowing for more focus on serious documentaries and news, without the constant concern of generating advertising revenue.

Most Popular TV Shows of 1970 [3]

1	Marcus Welby, M.D.	11	The Mod Squad
2	The Flip Wilson Show	12	Adam-12
3	Here's Lucy	13	Rowan & Martin's Laugh-In
4	Ironside	=	The Wonderful World of Disney
5	Gunsmoke	15	Mayberry R.F.D.
6	ABC Movie of the Week	16	Hee Haw
7	Hawaii Five-O	17	Mannix
8	Medical Center	18	The Men from Shiloh
9	Bonanza	19	My Three Sons
10	The F.B.I.	20	The Doris Day Show

[1] americancentury.omeka.wlu.edu/items/show/136.
[2] livinghistoryfarm.org/farminginthe50s/life_17.html.
[3] From the Nielsen Media Research 1970-'71 season of top-rated primetime television series in the USA.

Although sitcoms and variety programs remained popular in 1970, a new wave of intense TV dramas was keeping us glued to our television sets. A slew of police, detective and medical themed primetime TV programs hit our screens in the late '60s, and we were hooked.

Eight of the twenty top-ranking TV series for 1970 were medical or crime themed programs, most lasting well into the decade.

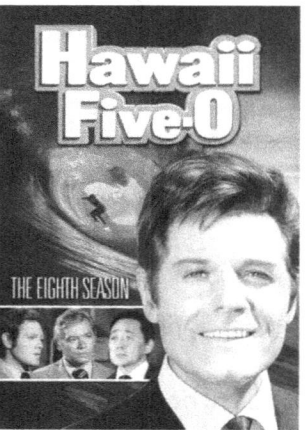

Jack Lord, Al Harrington, Kam Fong and James MacArthur in *Hawaii Five-O* (CBS. 1968-1980).

Airing for an impressive 12 seasons, *Hawaii Five-O* was largely shot on location in Honolulu, Hawaii. The show followed a special police task force fighting organized crime across the Hawaiian Islands.

The original series ended in 1980. A 2010 remake, based on the original series, ran for ten seasons.

Robert Young as Marcus Welby, with James Brolin as his head-strong young assistant and Elena Verdugo as their nurse, in *Marcus Welby, M.D.* (ABC. 1969-1976).

Valerie Harper, Edward Asner, Cloris Leachman, Gavin MacLeod, Mary Tyler Moore, and Ted Knight in *The Mary Tyler Moore Show* (CBS. 1970–1977).

Shirley Jones, David Cassidy, Susan Dey, Danny Bonaduce, Jeremy Gelbwaks & Suzanne Crough in *The Partridge Family* (ABC. 1970–1974).

The television networks were quick to turn out new programs to keep us tuning in. Here are a few of the new programs that aired for the first time in 1970: *The Mary Tyler Moore Show, The Partridge Family, The Odd Couple* and *Josie and the Pussycats*. Other notables include *McCloud, NFL Monday Night Football* and *The Goodies* (BBC, UK).

Josie and the Pussycats (CBS. 1970–1974).

Tony Randall and Jack Klugman in *The Odd Couple* (ABC. 1970–1975).

The "fat time of day:" you're really hungry and ready to eat two of everything. Here's how sugar can help.

"If sugar can fill that hollow feeling, I'm all for it."

The "fat time of day" is when you're over-hungry and want to overeat.

That's when your appestat* is turned up high. To turn your appestat back to low, take a little sugar in a soft drink, or a candy bar, shortly before mealtime.

Sugar turns into energy faster than any other food.

Sugar helps keep your appetite down, your energy up—and—helps slip you safely past the "fat time of day."

Sugar...only 18 calories per teaspoon, and it's all energy.

* "A neural center in the hypothalamus believed to regulate appetite." —Webster's Third New International Dictionary.

Advertisement

When you know what it takes to make a TEAC, you know why professional people wax lyrical about our A-7030.

This is a no-nonsense pro-quality tape deck, with unrivalled sound reproduction at 15 or 7½ ips. A streamlined solenoid control system for effortless operation. A system that makes cueing as easy as pushing a button. Automatic rewind and shutoff for built-in convenience.

The A-7030 is the sum of many systems, and the sum of our savvy in producing them. It's the head of our whole fine family of tape decks.

So if somebody wants to write a sonnet on it, we've got a great line for them.

Sounds like poetry to the pros.   A-7030

- Dual-speed hysteresis-synchronous motor for capstan drive. • Two heavy duty 6-pole capacitor-start induction motors for reel drive. • Tape tension adjustment. • Massive inertial flywheel, over 1½ pounds. • Instant off-the-tape monitoring without interruption of recording. • Sound-on-sound and echo with simple external connections. • Built-in mike-line mixer. • Stainless steel panel reinforced with 13/64" aluminum base plate for assured stable performance.

Sesame Street Hits Our Screens 1969–1970

When *Sesame Street* hit our screens, we had never seen anything quite like it before: a curriculum-based, engaging and educational children's program, using television as a learning tool. *Sesame Street* premiered in Nov 1969, airing its debut season throughout 1970.

Big Bird on the cover of *Time Magazine*, Nov 1970.

The original 1969-1970 Season 1 cast of *Sesame Street*.

American preschool children had been watching an average of 27 hours of television per week,[1] much of it unsuitable for young minds. The creators of *Sesame Street* sought to help prepare children for school, focusing on cultural diversity to reach disadvantaged children from the less prosperous non-white neighborhoods.

[1] en.wikipedia.org/wiki/History_of_Sesame_Street.

Educational advisors worked alongside the producers to develop the show's content. The show focused on children's cognitive skills as well as social and emotional development. Children were enlisted to test every episode for interest and engagement. If their attention wavered, the episode would be changed or abandoned.

Muppet characters created by designer Jim Henson (creator of the *Muppet Show*, 1976) could interact with human actors.

Lily Tomlin as Edith Ann, with Herry Monster in 1970.

Celebrity guests ensured that parents and older siblings would join the younger children to watch the show, and not switch to another station.

By the 50th anniversary of *Sesame Street*, an estimated 150 million children had watched 150 different versions of the show in 70 languages.

Over the years, Sesame Street has transformed for modern audiences. It is now available via TV, DVD, and CDs. It also has its own social media and YouTube channel.

1970 in Cinema and Film

As cinema-goers, our interests and focus had shifted away from traditional classic Hollywood standards, which were often bounding with optimism and happy endings. We were seeking movies that offered more depth, more pain and a sense of reality.

By 1970, fresh new directors like Francis Ford Coppola and Martin Scorsese demanded more artistic control. They bravely tackled darker, more gritty and more pessimistic themes of war, crime and depression. The era of big cinema houses owning their actors and controlling their directors had ended.

A new generation of brooding method-style actors rose to replace the retiring golden-era stars. Dustin Hoffman, Robert De Niro, Meryl Streep, Al Pacino, Jack Nicholson and Harvey Keitel are some of our enduring favorites.

Above: Dustin Hoffman and Faye Dunaway in *Little Big Man* (Warner Bros. 1970).

Left: Jack Nicholson and Karen Black in *Five Easy Pieces* (Columbia Pictures, 1970).

1970 film debuts

Susan Sarandon	Joe
Robert Downey, Jr.	Pound
Sissy Spacek	Trash
Danny DeVito	Dreams of Glass
Tommy Lee Jones	Love Story
Diane Keaton	Lovers and Other Strangers
Tom Selleck	Myra Breckinridge
Sylvester Stallone	The Party at Kitty & Stud's

* From en.wikipedia.org/wiki/1970_in_film.

Top Grossing Films of the Year

1	Love Story	Paramount	$106,397,000
2	Airport	Universal	$100,489,000
3	MASH	20th Century Fox	$67,300,000
4	Patton	20th Century Fox	$61,750,000
5	Woodstock	Warner Bros.	$50,000,000
6	Little Big Man	Warner Bros.	$31,560,000
7	Ryan's Daughter	MGM	$30,846,000
8	Tora! Tora! Tora!	20th Century Fox	$29,548,000
9	Chariots of the Gods	Constantin Film	$25,948,000
10	The Aristocats	Disney	$20,223,000

* From en.wikipedia.org/wiki/1970_in_film by box office gross in the USA.

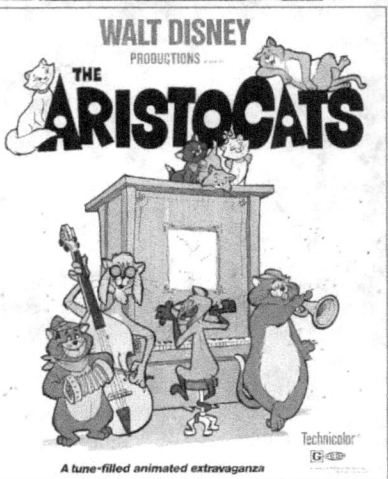

Based on Arthur Hailey's 1968 best selling novel, *Airport* was the first of many disaster-drama blockbusters of the '70s.

A Decade of Disasters

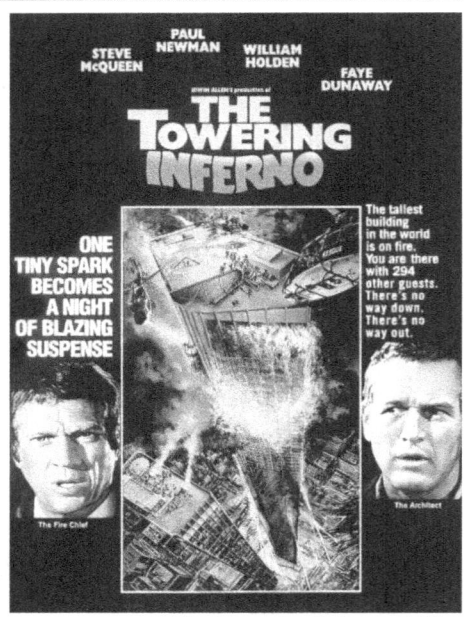

The Poseidon Adventure (20th Century Fox, 1972).

The Towering Inferno (20th Century Fox, 1974).

The decade of the '70s saw the disaster movie genre reign supreme at the box office. Large casts, multiple plot lines, life or death calamities and tales of survival kept us on the edge of our seats.

Earthquake (Universal, 1974).

Tidalwave (Toho, 1973).

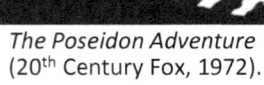

Advertisement

UP OFF YOUR KNEES, GIRLS. SHINYL VINYL, THE NO-WAX FLOOR IS HERE.

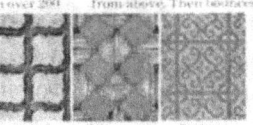

Up off your knees, girls. Shinyl Vinyl, the no-wax floor is here.

It has a built-in polished surface that takes the place of wax. Throw away your wax! Give up stripping down! Now there's Shinyl Vinyl from Congoleum in over 200 exciting floors, all with a beautiful No-Wax shine. To last the life of the floor. A finish that can't be greasy-gravied to death, or heeled-and-toed away. Even kids can't hurt it—it's that tough. And so is the sound-proofing cushion of foamed vinyl underneath. It "gives-in" under pressure from above. Then bounces back—to look brand new. Undented. Undaunted. A thing of beauty forever. Untouched by human knees.

Musical Memories

The start of the new decade brought sweeping changes in the world of music, as we trended away from the '60s psychedelic rock and silly love songs, towards the more mellow and serious vocals of a new generation of singer-songwriters. Kris Kristofferson, Cat Stevens, Elton John and Neil Diamond would lead this acoustic genre well into the '70s.

Also gaining in popularity was the less serious genre known as pop rock. The Jackson 5 dominated the charts in 1970 with 3 singles in the Billboard Top 20 Songs of the Year. Other favorites included the Carpenters, Bread, Linda Ronstadt and David Cassidy.

14th Jan– Diana Ross performed her final concert with the Supremes at the Frontier Hotel in Las Vegas. Five months later Ross released her debut solo album, titled *Diana Ross*, featuring her #1 hit single *Ain't No Mountain High Enough*.

10th Apr– Paul McCartney announced he was leaving The Beatles. During the same month their final album, *Let it Be*, was released, along with their final single, *The Long and Winding Road,* and a final film also titled *Let it Be*. By the end of the year all four former band members would separately release solo albums.

The third and last Isle of Wight, UK, Festival was held from 26th-31st August. More than 600,000 people came to hear The Who, Miles Davis, Chicago, The Doors, The Moody Blues, Supertramp, Kris Kristofferson, Joni Mitchell, Leonard Cohen, Jethro Tull and others perform. The festival's headline and star act, Jimi Hendrix, performed late on the last day. Sadly, he would be dead just two weeks later.

Although it was the largest and most ambitious event to date of its kind, it was a financial failure. Ticket sales underestimated the huge crowds who broke down fences to get in, heckling performers with unruly and often hostile behavior. It was a far cry from the peace and love atmosphere of 1969's Woodstock festival.

4th Jul– Casey Kasem's American Top 40 debuted on LA radio station KIIS.

25th Aug– Elton John performed his first US show at the Troubadour in Los Angeles.

18th Sep– Jimi Hendrix (aged 27) died in London whilst intoxicated with barbiturates.

4th Oct– Janis Joplin (aged 27) died of an accidental heroin overdose. Her 4th album, *Pearl*, released posthumously in 1971, topped the Billboard charts just 3 months later.

1970 Billboard Top 30 Songs

	Artist	Song Title
1	Simon & Garfunkel	Bridge Over Troubled Water
2	The Carpenters	(They Long to Be) Close to You
3	The Guess Who	American Woman
4	B.J. Thomas	Raindrops Keep Fallin' on My Head
5	Edwin Starr	War
6	Diana Ross	Ain't No Mountain High Enough
7	The Jackson 5	I'll Be There
8	Rare Earth	Get Ready
9	The Beatles	Let It Be
10	Freda Payne	Band of Gold

Diana Ross, 1968.

The Carpenters, 1st Aug 1972.

Simon and Garfunkel, 1968.

The Beatles *Let it Be* album cover, 1970.

	Artist	Song Title
11	Three Dog Night	Mama Told Me (Not to Come)
12	Ray Stevens	Everything Is Beautiful
13	Bread	Make It with You
14	Vanity Fare	Hitchin' a Ride
15	The Jackson 5	ABC
16	The Jackson 5	The Love You Save
17	Neil Diamond	Cracklin' Rosie
18	Dawn	Candida
19	Sly & the Family Stone	Thank You
20	Eric Burdon & War	Spill the Wine

The Jackson 5 on the *Ed Sullivan Show* (CBS. 14th Dec 1969).

21	Five Stairsteps	O-o-h Child
22	Norman Greenbaum	Spirit in the Sky
23	Melanie	Lay Down (Candles in the Rain)
24	The Temptations	Ball of Confusion
25	The Moments	Love on a Two-Way Street
26	The Poppy Family	Which Way You Goin' Billy?
27	Free	All Right Now
28	The Jackson 5	I Want You Back
29	Bobby Sherman	Julie, Do Ya Love Me
30	Sugarloaf	Green-Eyed Lady

* From the *Billboard* top 30 singles of 1970.

Advertisement

We used to think all a clock radio had to do was wake you up.
Then we woke up.

We used to think all a clock radio had to do was wake you up. Then we woke up.

In the beginning there was the clock radio. It woke you up but was hard to read.

Then came the Sony Digimatic Clock Radio. It was the first that woke you up and was easy to read.

Now there's something else. Sony Digimatic Clock Radios for the office. The living room. The kitchen. For almost anywhere.

Because now Digimatics with their big easy-to-read numbers that tell the time minute by minute come in a variety of shapes, sizes and styles.

Now that we've made the clock radio reading easy, we've made the clock radio choosing difficult.

Unless you want to get a Sony Digimatic for every room in the house.

SONY. Digimatic Clock Radios.

Advertisement

A Smith-Corona can help your teenager through college.
How many other graduation gifts can say that?

A Smith-Corona can help your teenager through college.
How many other graduation gifts can say that?

If your teenager is graduating from high school and heading to college, better forget the surfboards, skis, and cute little tape recorders. Because this fall he'll be up against the toughest, most competitive schooling known to man.

How about a gift that can help? A Smith-Corona Electric Portable.

Give him one and he can learn to type twice as fast as he now writes. And it'll be readable besides. His spelling can improve. His creative thinking gets a big boost. And he gets himself Organized, perhaps for the first time.

A Smith-Corona can make a difference to a college-bound teenager. We know because we've already helped quite a few.

Let your Smith-Corona dealer tell you more. He's in the Yellow Pages.

A Smith-Corona isn't a graduation gift that'll help a student have fun this summer. But it will help him get through college this fall.

Smith-Corona. The gift that helps.

Fashion Trends of the 1970s

By the early '70s, the fashion industry had lost its way, with designers and consumers alike seeking new directions and answers to the changing times. This was a decade without guidance and without rules. Trends caught on and shifted quickly. Fashions were varied and experimental. Pants got wider, skirts got shorter, and boots got taller. And within a season the trends reversed. Anything was possible, everything was acceptable.

Walking down any street you would have found skirts worn mini, midi, or full length. Pants could be slim-fit, wide, or bell bottomed, hip-hugging or waist-clinching. Tops might be tie-dye swirl-patterned or bold solids. Shirts came long and loose, or tight and tailored.

Daywear pants-suit and skirt-suit.

Dresses came in all shapes and lengths too. They could be short Mod shifts, or calico lace prairie-style. They could be tailored with shirt-style collars and buttoned-down fronts. They could be long and loose caftans, flowing maxi-dresses, or waisted tailored-cut with belts and A-line skirts taken straight from the '50s.

Patchwork maxi-dresses by Yves Saint Laurent.

The hippie and psychedelic fashions of the late '60s were adopted and modified by mainstream non-hippies into more elegant structured forms. Caftans, prairie dresses, patchwork fabrics, shawls, tassels and beads hit the runways, and the streets, in the early '70s.

Elizabeth Taylor during her bohemian period, 1969.

Maudie James models Thea Porter patchwork dress, 1970.

Weipert and Burda fashion show, 1972.

In contrast to the hippie trends, Mod dresses of the early '60s made a comeback. Space-age synthetics and plastics, widely used in the '60s, were replaced with comfortable cottons and stretch knits. In winter, tunic dresses could be worn over turtlenecks, with woolen stockings or thigh-high boots.

Mod mini dresses worn with white boots or shoes, early 1970s.

The '70s were the first full decade where pants for women gained mainstream acceptance, and we couldn't get enough of them. Pants could be worn for any occasion—pants-suits for the office, silky patterns for evenings, or blocks and geometrics dressed down for daywear. And let's not forget blue jeans, the staple of casual wear for both men and women.

Day wear pants from the Sears Spring/Summer catalog, 1970.

In the early '70s men and women wore their pants gently flared at the base. As the decade progressed, the flares got wider and wider, exploding into bell-bottoms by the mid-'70s.

Embroidered denim.   Flared knit polyester pants.   Flared silky jumpsuits.

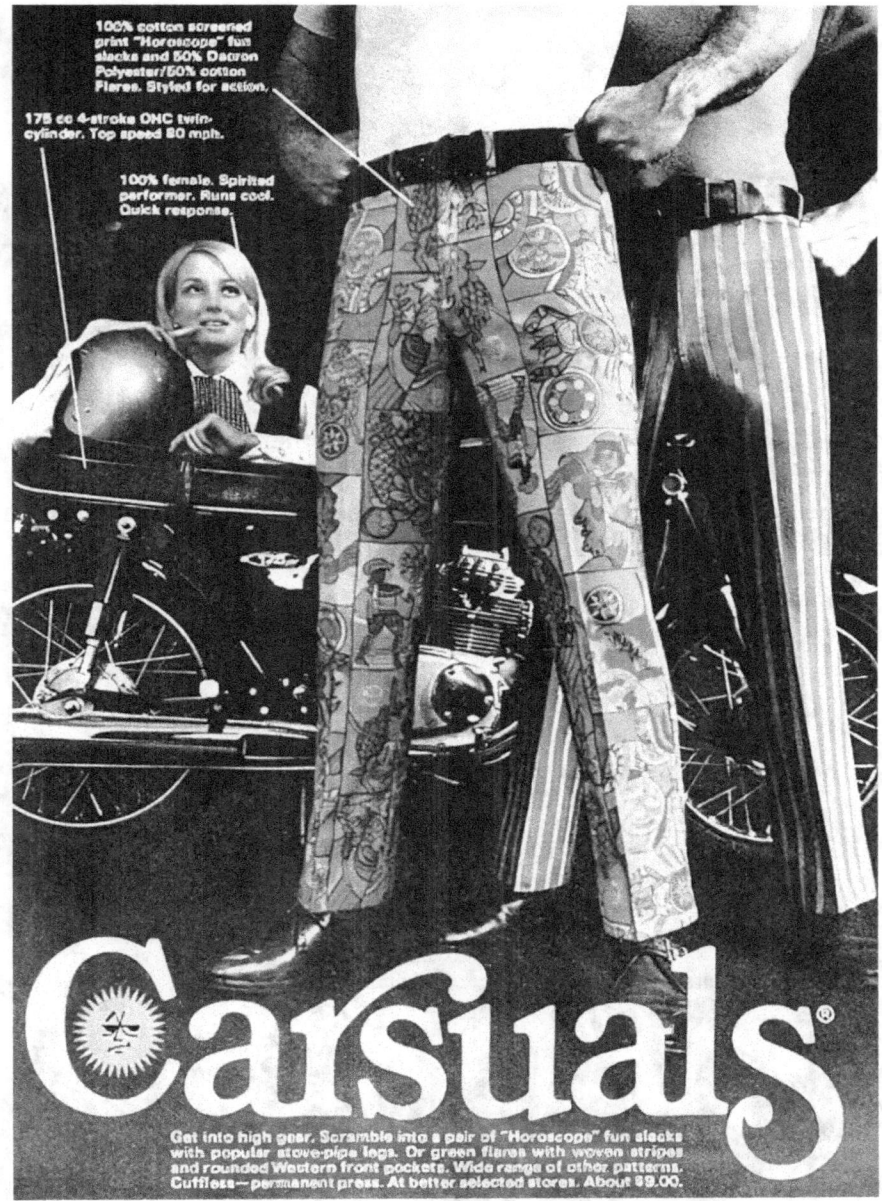

- 100% cotton screened print "Horoscope" fun slacks and 50% Dacron Polyester/50% cotton Flares. Styled for action. • 175 cc 4-stroke OHC twin-cylinder. Top speed 80mph. • 100% female. Spirited performer. Runs cool. Quick response.

Carsuals

Get into high gear. Scramble into a pair of "Horoscope" fun slacks with popular stove-pipe legs. Or green flares with woven stripes and rounded Western front pocket. Wide range of other patterns. Cuffless–permanent press. At better selected stores. About $9.00.

Shiny polyester Nik Nik shirts.

Stretch polyester tops and flared pants.

Terry toweling jumpsuits.

Caught between the hippie and mod fashion extremes of the early '70s, the rest of us settled for easy-care. Whether it was casual, formal or business attire, being easy to wash and drip-dry dictated what we wore. Non-iron wool jersey knits and non-iron polyester were the material of choice for men and women throughout the '70s.

The '70s are often considered to be the decade that fashion forgot (or the decade of fashion that we would rather forget). And it's not hard to see why. Anything and everything became acceptable, no matter how outlandish or mismatched.

Here are some of our more questionable fashion decisions from the decade.

Shiny stretch polyester jumpsuits.

Denim on denim.

Stretch knit pantsuits.

Safari suits.

John Travolta in *Saturday Night Fever* (Paramount Pictures, 1977).

Dancer at Studio 54, New York.

And then there was disco.
It shone so brightly. It glittered so briefly.
And in a flash, it was gone.

Sporting silver lamé jumpsuits.

Dancers at Studio 54, New York.

Model wears sequined jumpsuit.

An imaginative bag of
right-on things to wrap
around a body.
Colorful. Rebellious.
Daring.
And like that.
CAMPUS
EXPRESSIONS®

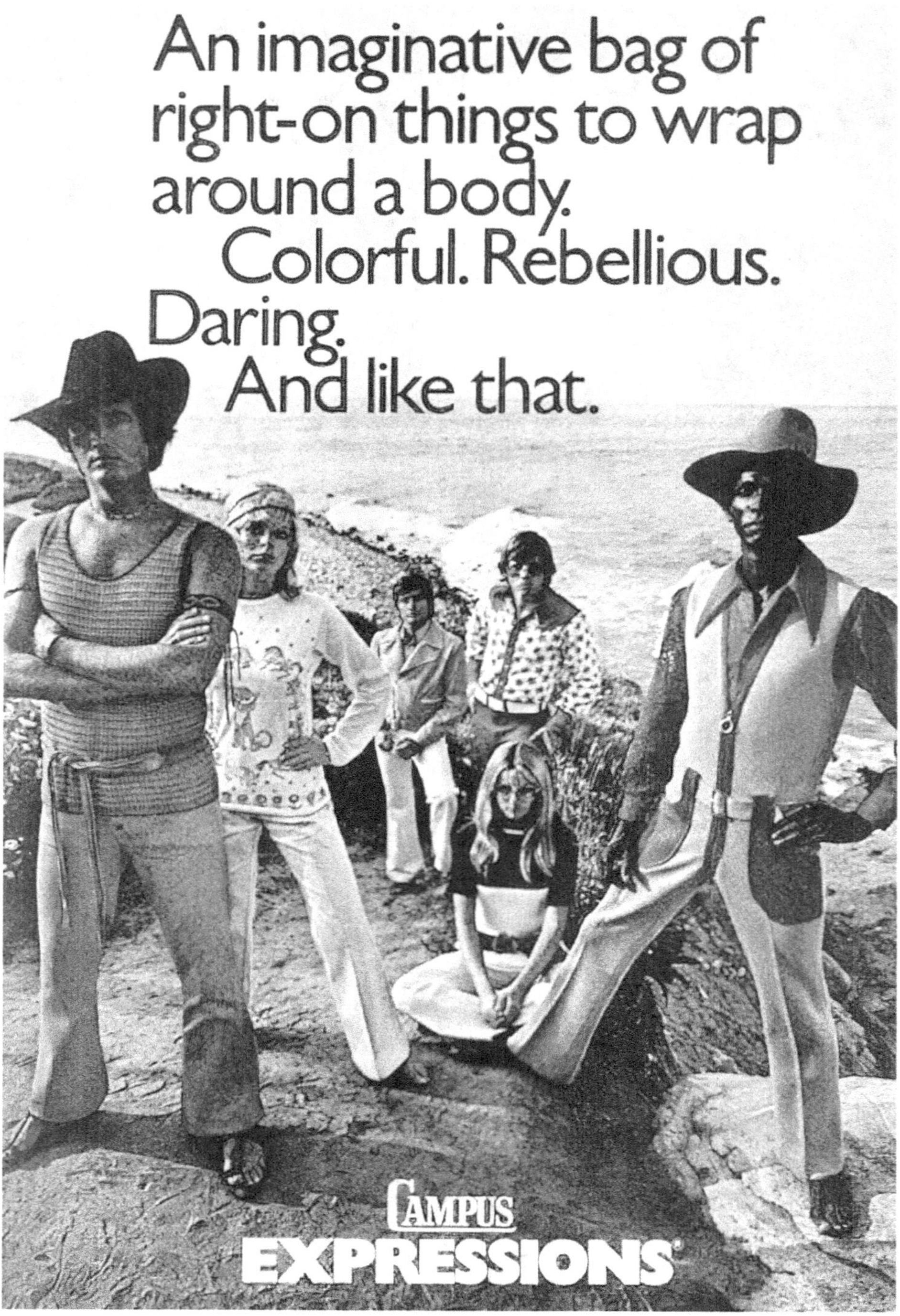

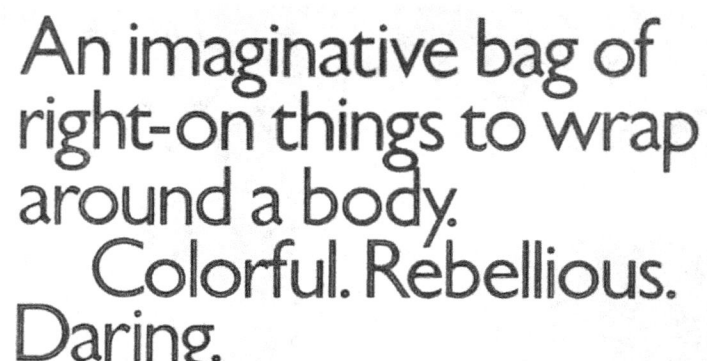

Advertisement

Poster for Elvis Presley's early concert tours in Las Vegas in 1970.

Schwarzenegger Wins Mr. Olympia   3rd October 1970

Arnold Schwarzenegger won his first professional body building title on 3rd October 1970 at New York's Town Hall. Beating defending title holder Sergio Oliva in a crowd-pleasing pose-for-pose final showdown, Schwarzenegger would go on the win the title six years in a row before retiring in 1975.

Austrian born Schwarzenegger had arrived in the USA just two years earlier to train and compete as a professional body builder, and to pursue his childhood dream of acting.

In 1969 Schwarzenegger secured his first movie role, *Hercules in New York*. His heavily accented voice was dubbed by another actor.

Future movie roles for which he is most famous include: *Conan the Barbarian* (1982), *The Terminator* (1984, with sequels in 1991, 2003 and 2015), *Total Recall* (1990) and *Kindergarten Cop* (1990).

In 2006 Schwarzenegger was elected Governor of California, a post which he held until 2010.

Over the years he has published several books on body building and in 2012 published his memoirs, *Total Recall: My Unbelievably True Life Story*.[1]

[1] Co-authored with Peter Petre.

British Commonwealth Games 16th–25th July 1970

The IX British Commonwealth Games was held in Edinburgh, Scotland, from 16th-25th July 1970. This was the first time HM Queen Elizabeth II attended as Head of the Commonwealth. It was also Scotland's first time to host the Games, the first time electronic photo-finish technology was utilized, and the first time metric units were used in all events.

The Games were immediately followed by the 1970 Commonwealth Paraplegic Games.

Raylene Boyle of Australia won 3 gold medals for the 100m sprint, 200m sprint and 4x100m relay. Boyle would go on to win more gold in the 1974 and 1978 Commonwealth games. She would later be inducted into the Athletics Australia Hall of Fame, made a Member of the Order of Australia, and named in Australia's Top 100 Sportswomen of All Time.

Don Quarrie of Jamaica won gold for the 100m sprint and 200m sprint, a feat he would replicate at the 1971 Pan American Games and 1974 Commonwealth Games. Regarded as one of athletics' greatest sprinters, Quarrie would go on to complete in five Olympic Games winning four gold medals.

Australian women dominated in the pool, winning gold in 12 of the 14 swim events. In addition, won a further 13 silver and bronze medals. 1383 athletes from 42 nations participated in 121 events. England won the most medals, with Australia bringing home the most gold.

Also in Sports

11th Jan– Kansas City Chiefs beat Minnesota Vikings 23-7 at Super Bowl IV, New Orleans.

Jan-Sep– Australian tennis legend Margaret Court won the Australian Open, French Open, Wimbledon and the US Open, to take the Grand Slam for 1970.

16th Feb– Joe Frazier won the heavyweight boxing title at Madison Square Gardens. He KOs Jimmy Ellis in 5 rounds.

Reigning champion Muhammad Ali had earlier been stripped of his title due to his resistance to the draft.

11th Feb– John Lennon paid £1,344 in fines for 96 students. The students had been arrested for anti-apartheid protests during the South African rugby tour of Scotland.

29th Mar– Manchester City (England) defeated Górnik Zabrze (Poland) in Vienna to take the 10th European Cup Winner's cup, 2-1.

2nd May– Diane Crump became the first woman jockey at the Kentucky Derby. Whilst she was ridiculed at the time, she is now considered a trail-blazer in the racing industry.

12th May– A new baseball record was set when Ernie Banks (Chicago Cubs), hit his 500th home run in Chicago's Wrigley Field.

21st Jun– Brazil won the FIFA World Cup Final, becoming the first team to win three times. At the same time, Brazilian forward Pelé became the first player to win the World Cup three times.

12th Jul– Jack Nicklaus beat Doug Sanders by 1 stroke at the British Open Men's Golf. It would be the second of his three Open Championships.

23rd Sep– The first New York Marathon was held attracting 127 entrants. Only 55 runners completed the event, held entirely within Central Park. Gary Muhrcke won with a time of 2:31:39. Winners received a wristwatch and recycled trophies.

14th Nov– 75 students, staff and supporters of the Marshall University football team died when their chartered plane crashed in West Virginia while returning from a game in North Carolina.

Advertisement

Time... most beautify told in 18K gold

Crafted completely in Switzerland by master watchmakers, every Corum is made of sold 18K gold... the same quality of fine gold used in the most expensive jewelry. Every diamond, ruby, emerald or sapphire in a Corum is alive with natural brilliance... no synthetics. The fully jeweled movement within takes six times longer to produce than ordinary watches. Invest a few dollars more and enjoy the lasting pride that comes from wearing a watch of exceptional quality with superior features.

Corum The watch of heirloom quality

Advertisement

"Heat and serve" isn't the best part (eating is).
The first time you bought a Banquet dinner you were looking for something quick and easy. Right?
Then you discovered (surprise!) that it was *good* too.
Maybe it is surprising that something as quick and easy as a frozen dinner can taste so good. Until you know the philosophy at Banquet: we think good food is more important than quick food. Or easy food. And we think you think so too.
Convenience and goodness make a great combination. But if we ever had to sacrifice one of them now you know which it would be.
Thank goodness for Banquet.

Other News from 1970

5th Mar– The Treaty on the Non-Proliferation of Nuclear Weapons came into effect. Aiming to prevent the spread of nuclear weapons, eventually leading to complete disarmament, it is now signed by 190 countries.

15th Mar-13th Sep– The World Fair was held in Osaka, Japan, with the theme "Progress and Harmony for Mankind". 70 countries participated, attracting 64 million visitors (a record not broken till the Shanghai World Expo in 2010). Major attractions included the first ever IMAX film, and a display of moon rock brought to earth by Apollo 12 astronauts in 1969.

23rd Mar– The United States Congress approved an amendment to the Constitution to lower the voting age from 21 to 18.

14th Apr– Debbie Reynolds quit her show in opposition to cigarette commercials being aired. Despite being the highest paid actress of her time, and commanding 42% of the viewing audience, Reynolds was concerned for the children watching her show.

22nd Apr– 23-year-old Gary Anderson won a design contest for a recycling logo to honor the first Earth Day. Still in use today, it has become one of the most recognizable logos of all time.

3rd May– The State Commission for Education in Mississippi voted to ban Sesame Street because it used "a highly integrated cast of children".

21st Jul– The Aswan High Dam across Egypt's Nile River was completed after eleven years of construction. Able to generate hydro-electricity, store water for irrigation and control flooding, the dam aimed to significantly aid Egypt's economy.

25th Aug– Farmers in Iceland blew up a small dam on the Laxá River. More than one hundred farmers claimed responsibility, yet none were charged. Their collective defiance successfully prevented the construction of a larger dam, which they claimed would have swept away their farms.

15th Dec– The Soviet's Venera 7 space probe became the first man-made probe to land on the surface of Venus and successfully transmit data. The probe survived a parachute failure and toppled over on landing. Its batteries expired twenty-three minutes later.

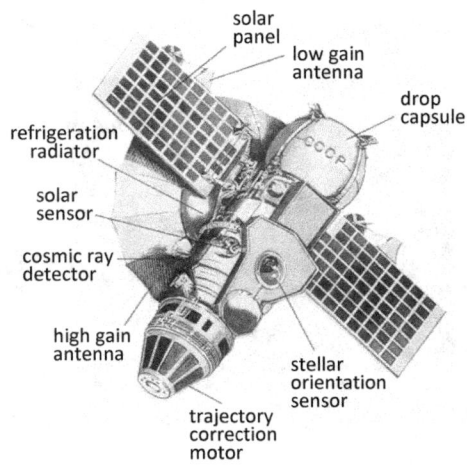

1970– Organic chemist John E. Franz discovered the herbicide glyphosate while working at Monsanto. The chemical became the active ingredient in Roundup, now a widely used weed killer.

1970– The US Senate Pill Hearings brought attention to the health risks associated with usage of birth control pills, resulting in mandatory side-effect disclosures to be included in the packaging–the first of its kind for any drug. Advocacy for women's health grew following the hearings.

Famous People Born in 1970

27th Jan– Carlos Javier Bernardo, Dutch prince.

29th Jan– Paul Ryan, American politician & Speaker of the House (2015-2018).

31st Jan– Minnie Driver, British actress & singer-songwriter.

3rd Feb– Warwick Davis, British actor.

9th Feb– Glenn McGrath, Australian cricketer.

7th Mar– Rachel Weisz, English actress.

18th Mar– Queen Latifah [Dana Owen], American rapper & actress.

28th Mar– Vince Vaughn, American actor.

4th Apr– Jason Stoltenberg, Australian tennis player.

19th Apr– Luis Miguel, Puerto Rican singer.

29th Apr– Andre Agassi, American tennis player.

29th Apr– Uma Thurman, American actress.

18th May– Tina Fey, American actress & comedian.

22nd May– Naomi Campbell, English model & actress.

25th May– Octavia Spencer, American actress.

15th Jun– Leah Remini, American actress.

16th Jun– Phil Mickelson, American golfer (5-time PGA Tour major winner).

19th Jun– Rahul Gandhi, Indian politician.

30th Jul– Christopher Nolan, English film director.

17th Aug– Jim Courier, American tennis player (4 Grand Slam singles titles, ranked #1 in 1992).

25th Aug– Claudia Schiffer, German supermodel & fashion designer.

26th Aug– Melissa McCarthy, comedian & actress.

27th Aug– Jim Thome, American baseball player & philanthropist (National Baseball Hall of Fame).

1st Sep– Padma Lakshmi, Indian model.

11th Sep– Taraji P. Henson, American actress & singer.

21st Sep– Samantha Power, Irish American author & diplomat (US Ambassador to the UN).

8th Oct– Matt Damon, American actor.

8th Oct– Sadiq Khan, British politician & 1st Muslim Mayor of London (2016).

9th Oct– Annika Sörenstam, Swedish golfer (10 LPGA major titles).

8th Nov– Tom Anderson, American co-founder of MySpace.

18th Nov– Megyn Kelly, American television news anchor & journalist.

1st Dec– Sarah Silverman, American actress & comedian.

12th Dec– Jennifer Connelly, American actress.

Advertisement

Smirnoff speaks in a whisper...

On a quiet afternoon, when the world stands still, and a five o'clock breeze blows fresh against your face. It's a moment as clear and crisp as a silver bell. In the Smirnoff life style, a time worth spending on cool thoughts and bright, free-wheeling dreams.

Smirnoff leaves you breathless®

Smirnoff speaks in a whisper...

On a quiet afternoon, when the world stands still, and a five o'clock breeze blows fresh against your face. It's a moment as clear and crisp as a silver bell. In the Smirnoff life style, a time worth spending on cool thoughts and bright, free-wheeling dreams.

Smirnoff leaves you breathless.

1970 in Numbers

Census Statistics [1]:

- Population of the world   3.7 billion
- Population in the United States   209.51 million
- Population in the United Kingdom   55.57 million
- Population in Canada   21.37 million
- Population in Australia   12.79 million
- Average age for marriage of women   20.8 years old
- Average age for marriage of men   23.2 years old
- Average family income USA $9,870 per year
- Minimum wage USA $1.60 per hour

Costs of Goods [2]:

- Average new house		$24,844
- Average new car		$3,430
- Chrysler Newport		$3,861
- A gallon of gasoline		$0.35
- Apples		$0.59 for 4 pounds
- A loaf of bread		$0.25
- A gallon of milk		$1.15
- Sirloin steak		$1.19 per pound
- Pork chops		$0.59 per pound
- Potatoes		$0.09 per pound
- Campbells tomato soup		$0.10
- Heinz ketchup		$0.19
- A cinema ticket		$1.55
- Head and Shoulders shampoo		$0.79

---

[1] Figures taken from worldometers.info/world-population, US National Center for Health Statistics, *Divorce and Divorce Rates* US (cdc.gov/nchs/data/series/sr_21/sr21_029.pdf) and United States Census Bureau, *Historical Marital Status Tables* (census.gov/data/tables/time-series/demo/families/marital. html).
[2] Figures from thepeoplehistory.com, mclib.info/reference/local-history & dqydj.com/historical-home-prices/.

Advertisement

Blow in her face and she'll follow you anywhere.

Hit her with tangy Tipalet Cherry. Or rich, grape-y Tipalet Burgundy. Or luscious Tipalet Blueberry. It's Wild!
Tipalet. It's new. Different. Delicious in taste and in aroma.
A puff in her direction and she'll follow you, anywhere.
Oh yes...you get smoking satisfaction without inhaling smoke.

Smokers of America, do yourself a flavor. Make your next cigarette a Tipalet.

New from Muriel. About 5 for 25¢.

Advertisement

Today A French Original Under $10.
Martell, a very special taste for people with very special tastes.

These words first appeared in print in the year 1970.

wish list

Agent Orange

Tourette's Syndrome

bioethics

anxiety disorder

first responder

zero waste

greener pastures

CONTROL FREAK

pro-life

Comfort food

X-rated

guilt trip

bad hair day

LOVE HANDLES

SLEEPING GIANT

Hot pants

*From merriam-webster.com/time-traveler/1970.

A heartfelt plea from the author:

I sincerely hope you enjoyed reading this book and that it brought back many fond memories from the past.

Success as an author has become increasingly difficult with the proliferation of **AI generated** copycat books by unscrupulous sellers. They are clever enough to escape copyright action and use dark web tactics to secure paid-for **fake reviews**, something I would never do.

Hence I would like to ask you—I plead with you—the reader, to leave a star rating or review on Amazon. This helps make my book discoverable for new readers, and helps me to compete fairly against the devious copycats.

If this book was a gift to you, you can leave stars or a review on your own Amazon account, or you can ask the gift-giver or a family member to do this on your behalf.

I have enjoyed researching and writing this book for you and would greatly appreciate your feedback.

Best regards,
Bernard Bradforsand-Tyler.

Please leave a book review/rating at:

https://bit.ly/1970-reviews

Or scan the QR code:

Flashback books make the perfect gift- see the full range at

https://bit.ly/FlashbackSeries

Image Attributions

Photographs and images used in this book are reproduced courtesy of the following:

Page 6 – From Seventeen Mag Feb 1970. Source: joyatri.com/joyatri-home-page/tag/ seventeen (PD image).*
Page 8 – Source: alex-harris.com/photography/may-day-1970.
Page 9 – Source: images from the U.S. News & World Report collection at the Library of Congress Prints and Photographs division. (PD image).
Page 10 – Advertisement source: ebay.com/itm/1972-Salem-Menthol-Cigarettes-Vintage-PRINT-AD-Tobacco-Smoking-Blond-Girl-1970s/264176008712. (PD image).*
Page 11 – Source: reddit.com/r/OldSchoolCool/comments/890bq6/ by u/Keakonu. Pre 1978, no renewed copyright. (PD image).*
Page 12 – Source: footage.framepool.com/shotimg/524716167. Pre 1978, no copyright mark (PD image) and jimmysirrelslove child.co.uk/fans/stoke-1970. Pre 1978, (PD image).
Page 13 – Women's Liberation protest 8th Nov 1971. Source: redflagwalks.wordpress.com/category/womens-liberation/. Pre 1978, no copyright mark (PD image). – Chelsea Street photo source: theguardian.com/football/ 2014/aug/10/footballs-glory-days-in-pictures by Gerry Cranham. Pre 1978, no copyright mark (PD image).
Page 14 – Images source unknown. Photographer unknown. Pre 1978, no copyright mark (PD image).
Page 15 – Postal workers strike in Hyde Park. Source: libcom.org/history/sorting-out-postal-strike-1971-joe-jacobs. Pre 1978, no copyright mark (PD image). – Women's Liberation protest outside Miss World contest, Albert Hall, 20th Nov 1970. Source: royalalberthall.com/about-the-hall/news/2014/november/miss-world-at-the-royal-albert-hall/. Pre 1978, (PD image). – North Ireland protests. Source: reddit.com/r/HistoryPorn/comments/98abcm/british_ soldiers_hold_back_civil_rights/ by u/NewRetroPepsi. Pre 1978, no copyright mark (PD image).
Page 16 – Commune members, source: allthatsinteresting.com/hippie-communes. – Tom and Pilar Law at Woodstock photo by Henry Diltz. Source: theguardian.com/music/gallery/2019/aug/15/woodstock-at-50-three-days-of-peace-pictures.
Page 17 – Tending to the fields, source: burlingtonfreepress.com/story/news/local/vermont/2015/07/24/ vermont-remains-hippie-epicenter/30564907/, photo by Rebecca Lepkoff of Vermont Historical Society. Pre 1978. – Geodesic dome, source: vpr.org/post/communes-hippie-invasion-and-how-1970s-changed-state#stream/0 by Kate Daloz. Pre 1978. – Commune bus, source: allthatsinteresting.com/hippie-communes. Pre 1978. No copyright mark (PD image).
Page 18 – Advertisement source: flickr.com/photos/nesster/47091578891. Attribution 4.0 Int (CC BY 4.0).
Page 19 – Source: vietnampeace.org/blog/antiwar-resistance-within-the-military-during-the-vietnam-war. Pre 1978, (PD image). – Jane Fonda, press conference 18 January 1975. Source: commons.wikimedia.org/wiki/File:Jane_Fonda_1975c by Mieremet.jpg, Rob / Anefo. From the Dutch National Archives (PD image).
Page 20 – Source: pinterest.com.au/pin/333196072430850347/. Pre 1978 (PD image).
Page 21 – Jeffrey Miller Shot At Kent State Protest, source: flickr.com/photos/33749589@N07/3634640610/, photo by John Filo. Attribution-ShareAlike 4.0 International (CC BY-SA 4.0). – Guardsmen face students, source: britannica.com/topic/Jackson-State-University. Pre 1978, no copyright mark (PD image). –Protest march source: wallstreetwindow.com/students-for-a-democratic-society-and-the-vietnam-war. Pre 1978, no mark (PD image).
Page 22 – Apollo 13 launch, source: images.nasa.gov/details-S70-34852, (PD image). – Apollo 13 crew, 10th &11th April 1970. Source: images-assets.nasa.gov/image/S70-36485/S70-36485~thumb.jpg, (PD image). – News papers 12th April 1970. Source: theatlantic.com/photo/2020/04/photos-50th-anniversary-apollo-13/609658/.
Page 23 – NASA engineers, source: images-assets.nasa.gov/image/as13-62-9004/as13-62-9004~thumb.jpg, (PD image). – Apollo 13 crew, source: images-assets.nasa.gov/image/S70-35614/S70-35614~thumb.jpg. (PD image).
Page 24 – Source: jpbtransconsulting.com/tag/marylin-bender/. Pre 1978, no copyright mark (PD image).
Page 25 – Boeing 747, source: commons.wikimedia.org/wiki/File:Boeing_747_rollout_(3).jpg. Pre 1978, no copyright mark (PD image). – Airport '77 film poster by Universal Pictures.**
Page 26 – Source: flickr.com/photos/andreboeni/32498848515/. Attribution 4.0 International (CC BY 4.0).
Page 27 – Source: flickr.com/photos/aussiefordadverts/5460184972/. Attribution 4.0 Int (CC BY 4.0).
Page 28 – Sources: vintageadbrowser.com/cars-ads-1960s/40 and vintageadbrowser.com/cars-ads-1970s/71.
Page 29 – Cobra source: flickr.com/photos/lightning72/4096977575/. Attribution 4.0 Int (CC BY 4.0).
– Vega source: commons.wikimedia.org/wiki/File:71_Chevrolet_Vega_Ad-Promo.jpg, (PD image).
Page 30 – Source: flickr.com/photos/91591049@N00/14660517292/. Attribution 4.0 International (CC BY 4.0).
Page 31 – Print magazine advertisement for Pontiac Bonneville. Source: eBay (PD image).*
Page 32 – Source: latimes.com/local/california/la-me-lopez-la-better-worse-20180825-story.html. Pre 1978. – Chart: epa.gov/transportation-air-pollution-and-climate-change/accomplishments-and-success-air-pollution-transportation.
Page 33 – Sources: insider.com/vintage-photos-los-angeles-smog-pollution-epa-2020-1. – commons.wikimedia.org /wiki/File:Two_California_Plaza_-_350_S._Grand_Avenue,_Los_Angeles.jpg.
– commons.wikimedia.org/wiki/File: EAST _RIVER_AND_MANHATTAN_SKYLINE_IN_HEAVY_SMOG_-_NARA_-_548365.jpg. – quora.com/What-does-the-British-phrase-it-was-a-real-pea-souper-mean. All (PD images).
Page 34 – NY Times cover 23rd April 1970. – Source: todayinhistory.tumblr.com/post/143215990635/april-22nd-1970-first-earth-day-on-this-day-in. Pre 1978 (PD image).

Page 36 – Print magazine advertisement for Las Vegas. Source: eBay (PD image).*
Page 37 – Stonewall protest, source: twitter.com/GBBranstetter/status/1232494830862790656. Pre 1978, no mark (PD image). – New York march, source: digitalcollections.nypl.org/items/510d47e3-af4e-a3d9-e040-e00a18064a99 from The New York Public Library Digital Collections. 1970. Pre 1978 (PD image). – Pride march in Kristiansands, Norway 2019 source: flickr.com/photos/larsverket/48611905288/ by Lars Verket, (PD image).
Page 38 – Advert source: flickr.com/photos/91591049@N00/24575016781. Attribution 4.0 Int (CC BY 4.0).
Page 40 – Still image and poster from the TV series Hawaii Five-0 by CBS, 1970.** – Marcus Welby MD cast, source: commons.wikimedia.org/ wiki/File:Marcus_Welby_MD_cast.JPG. Pre 1978, no mark (PD image).
Page 41 – The Mary Tyler Moore Show publicity image by CBS Television, 1970. Source: commons.wikimedia.org/ wiki/File:Mary_Tyler_Moore_cast_1970_1977.JPG. (PD image). – Jose and the Pussy Cats poster by Hanna-Barbera Productions.** – The Partridge Family publicity image by ABC Television Network. Source: commons.wikimedia. org/wiki/File:The_Partridge_Family_Cast_1972.jpg. (PD image). – The Odd Couple publicity image by Paramount Television. Source: en.wikipedia.org/wiki/The_Odd_Couple_ (1970_TV_series)#/media/File:Tony_Randall_Jack_ Klugman_Odd_Couple_1972.JPG. (PD image).
Page 42 – Print magazine advertisement for Sugar. Source: eBay (PD image).*
Page 43 – Teak 1971, source: flickr.com/photos/nesster/5789831696/. Attribution 4.0 Int (CC BY 4.0).
Page 44 & 45 – Time magazine cover by Bill Pierce, Nov 1970.** – Sesame Street original cast, 1970. Source: reddit.com/r/ OldSchoolCool/comments/9lg13v/the_original_sesame_street_cast_c_1970/ by u/DenMother8. – Debut Episode, source: calendar.songfacts.com/november/10/17635. – Lily Tomlin, source: muppet.fandom.com/wiki/Herry_Monster. Reproductions included here for information only under U.S. fair use laws due to: 1- No free alternative can exist of trademarked characters; 2- images are low resolution copies and are too small for reproduction; 3- images do not limit the copyright owner's rights to profit from the works; 4- The images are significant to the article created.
Page 46 – Still images from the films *Little Big Man* by Cinema Center Films,** and *Five Easy Pieces* by BBS Productions.**
Page 47 – Film posters** for the movies *Airport* by Universal, *Love Story* by Paramount, and *The Aristocats* by Disney.
Page 48 – Film posters** for the movies *The Poseidon Adventure* by 20th Century Fox, *The Towering Inferno* by 20th Century Fox, *Earthquake* by Universal Pictures, and *Tidalwave* by Toho.
Page 49 – 1970 Congoleum vinyl floor advertisement. Pre 1978, no copyright mark (PD image).
Page 50 – The Supremes promotional photo by GAC in 1967. Source: commons.wikimedia.org/wiki/File:The_ Supremes_1967.JPG. (PD image). – The Beatles Magical Mystery Tour press photo. Source: commons. wikimedia.org/wiki/File:The_Beatles_magical_mystery_tour.jpg, licensed under Creative Commons Attrib 3.0.
Page 51 – Elton John, source: fineartamerica.com/featured/elton-john-1970-3-chris-walter.html?product =poster,1970. – Janis Joplin 18 April 1969 in New York City by Elliot Landy, source: commons.wikimedia.org/wiki/File:Janis_ Joplin_in_1969.png, licensed under the Creative Commons Attribution-Share Alike 4.0 International. – Jimi Hendrix 24th May 1967, Stockholm, Sweden. Source: commons.wikimedia.org/wiki/File:Jimi_Hendrix_1967_uncropped.jpg.
Page 52 – Diana Ross, source: it.wikipedia.org/wiki/The_Supremes (PD image). – Simon and Garfunkel 1968, source: commons.wikimedia.org/wiki/File:Simon_and_Garfunkel_1968.jpg (PD image).
Page 53 – Still image from the Jackson 5 on the Ed Sullivan Show,** source: mjvibe.com/ed-sullivan-shows-on-youtube-including-the-jackson-5/.
Page 54 – Source: vintageadbrowser.com/electronics-ads-1970s/2. Pre 1978 (PD image).
Page 55 – Source: ebay.com/itm/1971-AD-SMITH-CORONA-TYPEWRITER-GRADUATE-MOPED-SPORTS-GEAR/ 352906287093. Pre 1978 (PD image).
Page 56 – Pants and skirt-suit, 1969, creator unknown. Pre 1978, (PD image).– Maxi-dress by YSL, Spring-Summer 1969. Source: minniemuse.com/articles/creative-connections/patchwork. Pre 1978, (PD image).
Page 57 – Elizabeth Taylor, source: instyle.com/celebrity/transformations/elizabeth-taylors-changing-looks. – Thea Porter dress, photographer Patrick Hunt, 1970. – Weipert and Burda fashion show, Apr 1972, photo by Friedrich Magnussen. Permission CC BY-SA 3.0 DE. – Mini dresses, sources: pinterest.com/pin/ 99782947967669796/ & flickr.com/photos/33158682@N06/5285970751/. Pre 1978, (PD image).
Page 58 – Fashions from Sears Catalogues, pre-1978, no copyright mark (PD image). – Hungarian singer Szűcs Judit wears embroidered demin. Source: commons.wikimedia.org/wiki/File:Szűcs_Judit_énekesnő._ Fortepan_88657.jpg. Licensed under the Creative Commons Attribution-Share Alike 3.0 Unported. – Dacron pants from the 1975 J.C. Penney catalog. Pre 1978, (PD image).
– Flared jumpsuits, creator unknown. Pre-1978, (PD image).
Page 59 – Source: advertisingarchives.co.uk/en/page/show_home_page.html. Pre-1978, (PD image).
Page 60 – Nik Nik shirts, polyester jumpsuits, and knit pantsuits, source: onedio.com/haber/erkekte-retro-modasinin-tutmamasinin-32-mantikli-sebebi-300983. – Polyester tops and pants, toweling jumpsuits, and shrink tops by Colombia Minerva, source: flashbak.com/the-good-the-bad-and-the-tacky-20-fashion-trends-of-the-1970s-26213/. – Denim on denim source: typesofjeanfits.com/a-brief-history-of-jeans-denim-history-timeline/. – Safari suits source: klyker.com/1970s-fashion/. All images this page pre-1978, no copyright mark or renewal (PD image).
Page 61 – Still image from the film *Saturday Night Fever* by Paramount Pictures.** Source: vocal.media/beat/ the-list-saturday-night-fever-40th-anniversary. – Dancers at *Studio 54*, sources: definition.org/studio-54/2/ and alexilubomirski.com/image-collections/ studio-54. Pre 1978 (PD images).

Page 62 – Source: flickr.com/photos/91591049@N00/48487751622/ by Campus Expressions, 1971. Attribution (CC BY 4.0).
Page 63 – Elvis promotional poster from 1970.**
Page 64 – Source: schwarzenegger.it/galleria/muscle1.html. Pre 1978, no copyright mark (PD image). – *Conan the Barbarian* promotional poster by Universal Studios.**
Page 66 – Margaret Court source: tennis.com/pro-game/2014/01/twenty-four-majors-good/50047/. Pre 1978, (PD image). – Frazier vs Ellis source: si.com/boxing/2011/11/08/08joe-fraziers-biggest-fights#&gid=ci0255c87c80422515&pid=frazier-ellis-i. Pre 1978, (PD image).
– Diane Crump, source: washingtonpost.com/history/ 2019/05/04/kentucky-derbys-first-female-jockey-ignored-insults-boycott-threats-she-just-wanted-ride/
Page 67 – First NY marathon by Don Hogan Charles source: gearpatrol.com/outdoors/a349113/tips-for-running-your-first-marathon/.
Page 68 – 1970 Corum 18k Gold Switzerland Watch Print Ad. Pre 1978, no copyright mark (PD image).
Page 69 – 1970 Banquet Fried Chicken Frozen TV Dinner Food Ad. Pre 1978, no copyright mark (PD image).
Page 70 – Osaka World fair photos source: metaformdesigninternational.com/#/1970-osaka/. Pre 1978, no copyright mark (PD image). – Gary Anderson photo source: en.wikipedia.org/wiki/Recycling_symbol. Pre 1978, (PD image).
Page 71 – Aswan High Dam photo source: commons.wikimedia.org/wiki/File:AswanHighDam_Egypt.jpg, licensed under the Creative Commons Attribution-Share Alike 3.0. – slicethelife.com/2020/02/16/hans-remembers-monday-february-16-1970-50-years-ago. Pre 1978, (PD image).
Page 72-74 – All photos are, where possible, CC BY 2.0 or PD images made available by the creator for free use including commercial use. Where commercial use photos are unavailable, photos are included here for information only under U.S. fair use laws due to: 1- images are low resolution copies; 2- images do not devalue the ability of the copyright holders to profit from the original works in any way; 3- Images are too small to be used to make illegal copies for use in another book; 4- The images are relevant to the article created.
Page 75 – 1970 Smirnoff Vodka Advertisement, 1950. Source: flickr.com/photos/91591049@N00/ 40669736013/ by SenseiAlan. Attribution 4.0 International (CC BY 4.0).
Page 78 – Print magazine advertisement for Tipalet. Source: eBay (PD image).*
Page 79 – Print magazine advertisement for Martell. Source: eBay (PD image).*

*Advertisement (or image from an advertisement) is in the public domain because it was published in a collective work (such as a periodical issue) in the US between 1925 and 1977 and without a copyright notice specific to the advertisement.
**Posters for movies or events are either in the public domain (published in the US between 1925 and 1977 and without a copyright notice specific to the artwork) or owned by the production company, creator, or distributor of the movie or event. Posters, where not in the public domain, and screen stills from movies or TV shows, are reproduced here under USA Fair Use laws due to: 1- images are low resolution copies; 2- images do not devalue the ability of the copyright holders to profit from the original works in any way; 3- Images are too small to be used to make illegal copies for use in another book; 4- The images are relevant to the article created.

This book was written by Bernard Bradforsand-Tyler as part of *A Time Traveler's Guide* series of books.

All rights reserved. The author exerts the moral right to be identified as the author of the work.

No parts of this book may be reproduced, stored in any retrieval system, or transmitted in any form or by any means, without prior written permission from the author.

This is a work of nonfiction. No names have been changed, no events have been fabricated. The content of this book is provided as a source of information for the reader, however it is not meant as a substitute for direct expert opinion. Although the author has made every effort to ensure that the information in this book is correct at time of printing, and while this publication is designed to provide accurate information in regard to the subject matters covered, the author assumes no responsibility for errors, inaccuracies, omissions, or any other inconsistencies herein and hereby disclaims any liability to any party for any loss, damage, or disruption caused by errors or omissions.

All images contained herein are reproduced with the following permissions:
- Images included in the public domain.
- Images obtained under creative commons license.
- Images included under fair use terms.
- Images reproduced with owner's permission.

All image attributions and source credits are provided at the back of the book. All images are the property of their respective owners and are protected under international copyright laws.

First printed in 2020 in the USA (ISBN 979-8672961163).
2nd Ed 2021 (978-0-6450623-8-0), 3rd Ed 2024 (XXXXXXXX).
Self-published by B. Bradforsand-Tyler.

www.ingramcontent.com/pod-product-compliance
Lightning Source LLC
Chambersburg PA
CBHW072105110526
44590CB00018B/3316